Shortcut to a Positive Mental Attitude

A powerful self-improvement booklet to positive thinking

For Mal & DomiQ
Positive thinking is a joy forever

Introduction

What is the true path to happiness? To some, it's riches and wealth or satisfying material needs; to others, it's being content and leading a good life. Either way, both require a positive state of mind - a positive mental attitude to bring you all you desire and more.

> *"Not that I am speaking of being in need, for I have learned in whatever situation I am to be content. I know how to be brought low, and I know how to abound. In any and every circumstance, I have learned the secret of facing plenty and hunger, abundance and needI can do all things through him who strengthens me. Philippians 4:11-13*

To stay on the path of happiness, adapt an attitude of positive thinking. Use it consciously in everything you do, with every person that crosses your path and in every thought that enters your mind.

It all begins and ends in your mind. What you give power to has power over you.

Leon Brown

I.

If you woke up this morning and decided to put the positivity back into your life, then this booklet is for you. But first a word of warning - Only read on if you are serious about developing positive thinking. For if your goal is purely one of curiosity, I urge you to put down this booklet

 go find something else to read - perhaps Alice in

Wonderland might just be what you're looking

for.

However, if you have decided to read on, I would

like to congratulate you in making the best

decision that you've probably made in a long

time. For in doing so, you are about to change

your life.

Simply follow the steps given and you will see

that this way is so much easier than anything you

will have perhaps encountered before.

All I ask is that you do not start lightly. Commit

to the process described herein and I promise you, you will develop a positive mental attitude. I also encourage you to take your time when going through the next few pages. I totally understand your eagerness to cut to the chase, but in doing so, you will not gain anything. After all, it's taken this long to come across this little gem, and it definitely won't be of any benefit to you if you rush to the finish.

Now before we get started, take a moment to think about what it is you really want to get out of life now, today, from this day on. I'm not saying dream the impossible, such as winning the national lottery, for you must know by now that the chances of being run over (heaven forbid) by a bus are higher. No, I'm talking about changing your circumstances; changing your behaviour to yourself and towards others; and changing the way you are perceived by others. Of course, you'll be thinking,"been there, done that...", but believe me, everything you've tried and tested, and failed at, has failed because you have not sustained the required behaviour. You tripped up at some point [+] decided (on a subconscious level) the whole thing was never going to work [=] end results. Well, what's different about this? I hear you ask. Nothing! Absolutely nothing. For with this method there are no hitches except your state of mind. Believe it or not, it's not the thoughts that count but what we do with them. So developing a positive mental attitude ensures your thoughts remain kind, positive, optimistic and constructive. You'll be resetting your mind, if you like, to draw good to yourself and fend off all things undesired. Above all is, you'll be deciding on which path you are going to walk from this day forward. The very fact that you have decided to read this booklet and not Alice in Wonderland, says it all. And if at this very moment, you are in doubt in any shape or form, I once again urge you to PUT it down, and come

back to it at a time when you feel you are truly

ready to make a change.

II.

Ok. Since you've decided to go for it - it's important for you to know that you have committed to a clear and definite plan for bettering your life.

The process is uncomplicated and very straightforward and it is my sincere belief that this will change your thinking and the way people see you. It will generate unmeasurable success in ways in which you'll kick yourself for not having come across this booklet before. This, of course, is not strictly true, for it would have been impossible for you to have discovered this booklet before now. As the saying goes nothing happens before time and it is your time to discover how your mind can change your life for the better, starting today.

> ## Each person is born
> ## with an infinite power,
> ## against which no
> ## earthly force is of the
> ## slightest significance.
> Neville Goddard

III.

Most people are unaware of their power. So

there is a fair chance that you are one of the

many people that think an outside source is

responsible for your thoughts. However, I want

you to realise and accept that it is you. You are

the operator; you are in the driving seat. There is no great force taking control of your mind. It is you and only you.

Having said that, it's important to stress how vulnerable our minds are. There are forces feeding it, but how we react is entirely up to us. Let me give you an example: I'm very suggestible, so if I see an advertisement for a bar of chocolate, I will go out and buy that bar of chocolate. However if I stop and put my brain into gear first(take time to think about it), I might realise I don't actually want any chocolate. I then make the decision to not buy that bar of chocolate - I win. Are you with me? Good. That was easy. So let me give you another example: On my way to the coffee machine, I pass two colleagues talking and laughing. As I approach their smiles drop and they stop talking. I begin to feel uncomfortable. Within a split second several thoughts (positive and negative) have gone through my head including the most common one..., "they must be talking about me". The big question here is, which thought do I hold on to?

I decide not to stop and join the conversation. Instead I nod my head politely and carry on about my business. My mind now embarks on a journey of how "I don't have time to chat" and

"I've never liked the look of those too anyways".

Get the point?

Of course, I could easily have chosen to

think ,"they could be talking about something

that is none of my business" and spared myself a

lot of aggravation.

However, nine out of ten times, we tend to go

for the most destructive thought because

according to psychologists, the brain is hard-

wired to register and remember negative things.

The fact is we tend to give little thought to

most of our daily thoughts (and we have

thousands and thousands of them every day).

We don't have to hold on to them all - but the ones we hold on to can make a real difference.

How we react to things, how we feel or what we have today, all come from the thoughts and feelings we have harboured in the past or are harbouring now.

So how do we change our lives? We flick the switch and disempower our negative thoughts and conditions; by refusing to give them 'air time'. We stop them from going round time after time in our heads, like records played over and over again on the radio. In other words, we train our minds to focus on the positive things.

Over the next few pages, I am going to give you

specific instructions for what you must do to change your life for the better. If you follow these instructions, you will develop a positive mental attitude and the results will be truly startling. You will see the difference if not today, then tomorrow, next week, next month, even next year.

Before moving on though, I would like to ask one small favour - one that you must only fulfil if you can wholeheartedly say you have followed all the steps given and can truly testify to the results. Don't be alarmed or put off by this, it's simply a request to spread the word. I'll come back to this later. In the meantime, if you are ready to change your life forever - let us begin.

IV.

These instructions are not for the simple mind

for you are about to train yourself in the habit

of thought control. You are going to realise that

you really can choose your thoughts and your

moods.

To do so, you must follow all the steps given in order to establish a fixed system of conditioning your mind to remain positive at all times. Deviate and you will fail! Persevere and it will pay off! To ensure that you remain positive at all times you must be vigilant and on your guard. You will need to step out of your comfort zone and relinquish all thoughts of fear and anxiety. You must simply trust the process. Know that it is not wise to reason why for the only secret here is when you change your mind, your condition and environment changes too. It is law!

V.

To ensure your thoughts remain positive, constructive, optimistic, and kind:

1. Start each day with a positive thought: as soon as you open your eyes give thanks for the night that has passed (whether you slept well or not) and acknowledge how much you are looking forward to a brand new day

2. Be agreeable to other people's state of mind and difficulties at all times so as to get along with them. Avoid reacting to trivialities, which in turn stops small things from becoming major issues. Don't get drawn in - bring out the positive in people by asking questions, such as, 'How can I help you?'

3. Go out of your way to be enthusiastic and give

   compliments - express yourself in a friendly

   tone.

   If need be, avoid people who always annoying

   or negative - even if they are friends or

   family, for such people are sure to lead you

   astray

4. Turn every problem into a challenge. Look for

   solutions by focusing on what you can do.

   There is always some action you can take.

   Then give thanks and look for the pearls of

   wisdom for every experience should pay off

   one way or another - real strength grows out

   of real struggles

5. Do not react to criticism. Accept it and use it for self-examination: work out how much of it is justified then use it to make changes. Be sure to focus solely on things you can change. For only two things in life cause worry - things you can do something about and things you can't

6. When feeling sorry for yourself look around for others who are worse off than you, and (offer to) do something for them

7. When faced with negative news in the media, do not dwell on it, think about something positive for at least five minutes afterwards. In fact, go the other way and make it a habit

to find something funny to laugh at each day.
Laugh at irritations, and things that make you
angry (but for obvious reasons, don't do this
in people's faces)

8. Remain open-minded at all times. Exercise
patience and generosity

9. Take five, and sit still for at least five
minutes each day. Use it for example, to think
only of things which you desire most

10. Get a good night's sleep (6-8 hours) and
exercise regularly. Try to eat at least three
square meals a day, for a healthy body is a
healthy mind

As creatures of habit, we love routine. So in order to succeed, you must make these instructions your daily routine. Try to keep this up for seven days straight.

Read them and put them into practice morning, noon and night.

If you miss a day you must start again until you achieve seven days in a row. If you are reading the e-book, it may be useful to know that the printed version has a checklist/notes section at the back of the book so you can physically record progress). Once you've accomplished your first seven days, move on to the next seven,

which will be easier than the first. If you miss a

day during the second week, go back to the

beginning of the second week and so on.

The longer you exercise the process, the easier

it gets. Know that your success is based entirely

on your attitude, your commitment and self-

discipline. You are the only person who can

generate a new mindset. So, allow no-one or

nothing to pollute your mental environment.

 Impress upon your mind that if you believe it,

you can achieve it and give thanks every day for

having complete control over your own mind.

Over time, you will find that the process of

renewing your life **will** have started and you **will** experience a transformation that **will** change your life forever. This method works in accordance with the laws of the universe, so it cannot fail. Mental consent constitutes thoughts - it's not the thoughts but what we do with them what counts. So turn away from negative thoughts, do not dwell on any of them at any time and when struggling to stay on track simply refuse to accept anything at face value.

Challenges in the beginning suggests things are moving - and if you have spiritual understanding, you will be well-equipped to deal with them.

It's worth noting that if your mind tries to
deceive you, your heart will tell you the truth.
Once the period of instability passes, the results
will appear - your mood and your mindset **will**
change.

When you're convinced you have achieved a
positive mental attitude, I would like to ask of
you that favour I mentioned earlier:

As your soul is your secret place within, keep
this process to yourself until you start yielding
the results. Then, once you are truly convinced
that your positive thinking is helping you

successfully deal with any obstacles you encounter in life, please tell others, so they can experience the same - for sharing is caring.

Better still, gift them their own copy of this booklet and hold on to yours.

Without a doubt, this little booklet will serve as a constant reminder - to those who own it - that a positive mental attitude really does rest in the hands and mind of the beholder.

****

Checklists & Notes

The following pages contain checklists, which you can use to keep to track of your efforts and ensure your thoughts remain positive, constructive, optimistic, and kind. It's best to fill them in at the end of the day after you have had the chance to put the exercises into practice. There is also a notes section, which you can use as a journal to record your successes. Remember, trust the process!

Notes:

"Many of life's failures are people who did not realise how close they were to success when they gave up." –Thomas Edison.

Week

Day	1	2	3	4	5	6	7

1. Today I started my day with positive thoughts

2. Today I was agreeable at all times

3. Today I saw all my problems as challenges

4. Today I did not react to criticism

5. Today I helped others instead of feeling sorry for myself

6. Today I found something to laugh at

7. Today I was open minded

8. Today I took 5 minutes for myself

9. Today I exercised and/or ate well

10. I love and approve of myself

Notes:

"Just because you fail once doesn't mean you're gonna fail at everything." — Marilyn Monroe.

Week

	Day	1	2	3	4	5	6	7

1. Today I started my day with positive thoughts

2. Today I was agreeable at all times

3. Today I saw all my problems as challenges

4. Today I did not react to criticism

5. Today I helped others instead of feeling sorry for myself

6. Today I found something to laugh at

7. Today I was open minded

8. Today I took 5 minutes for myself

9. Today I exercised and/or ate well

10. I love and approve of myself

Notes:

"Patience and perseverance have a magical effect before which difficulties disappear and obstacles vanish." – John Quincy Adams.

Week

Day	1	2	3	4	5	6	7

1. Today I started my day with positive thoughts

2. Today I was agreeable at all times

3. Today I saw all my problems as challenges

4. Today I did not react to criticism

5. Today I helped others instead of feeling sorry for myself

6. Today I found something to laugh at

7. Today I was open minded

8. Today I took 5 minutes for myself

9. Today I exercised and/or ate well

10. I love and approve of myself

Notes:

"It always seems impossible until it's done." – Nelson Mandela

Week

Day	1	2	3	4	5	6	7
1. Today I started my day with positive thoughts							
2. Today I was agreeable at all times							
3. Today I saw all my problems as challenges							
4. Today I did not react to criticism							
5. Today I helped others instead of feeling sorry for myself							
6. Today I found something to laugh at							
7. Today I was open minded							
8. Today I took 5 minutes for myself							
9. Today I exercised and/or ate well							
10. I love and approve of myself							

About this book

This booklet is a very powerful self-help booklet on positive thinking.

The market is full of books of old thinkers with new thought and new thinkers with old thought and all the information out there is as valid and valuable as it is and was when it was produced. However, the author feels those in need of a quick fix - in this case to positive thinking - could benefit greatly from this little booklet. For if we are to believe what's out there, you don't need to spend years trying to yield results. It's here now, yours for the taking today.

Shortcut to a Positive Mental Attitude is just one of a series to come offering shortcuts to unlocking some of the well-known secrets of the universe.